Ladybird  Readers

Is it Nat?

Series Editor: Sorrel Pitts
Story by Catherine Baker
Illustrated by Chris Jevons

Ladybird Readers Starter Level

Title		Phonics	Sight Words
1	Alphabet Book	A—Z	
2	Is it Nat?	s a t p i n	a is it
3	Nat Sits		an in sit
4	Top Dog and Pompom	m d g o c k	and can I into no
5	Top Dog is Sick		got not
6	The Fun Run	e u r h b f l	at get go has off the to up
7	Gus is Hot!		full his of on put
8	Jazz the Vet	j v w x y z qu	be but had he him she tell was
9	Vick the Vet		did well will
10	Dash and Thud	ch sh th ng	if ran then they with yes
11	Big Bad Bash		big long that this
12	The Big Fish	ai ee oa oo	her look see them
13	The Big Ship		let me my too
14	Martin and Lorna	ar or ur ow oi er	all are for
15	Farmer Carl		cut down good help now
16	The Big Dipper	igh ear air ure	as have like said some went you
17	The Silver Ring		come from so stop we what

First, go through the phonemes on page 4, and do the activity on page 5. Then, read the words in the first half of the book, focusing on pronunciation and blending.

The sight words are introduced in the second half of the book, first on their own and then in full sentences.

At the back of the book, there are activities and assessments practicing phonemes and sight words. These icons indicate the key skills required in each activity:

 Spelling and writing   Speaking   Reading

Is it Nat?

Look at the story

First, look at the words and pictures.
Use the words to practice phonics.

Phonics focus

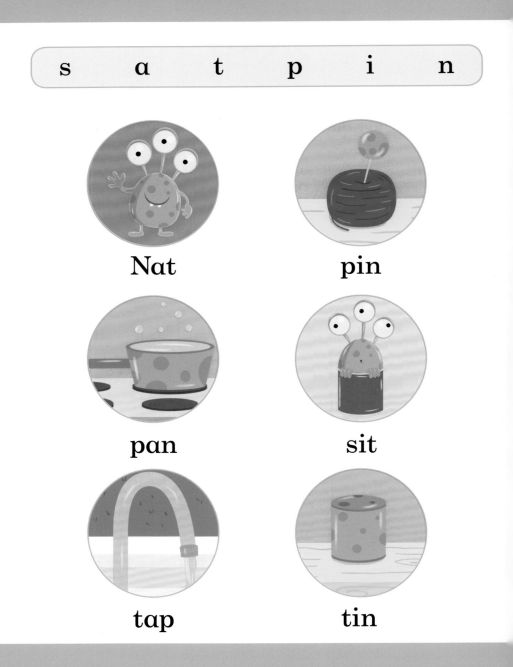

s a t p i n n

Nat

pin

pan

sit

tap

tin

Aa Bb Cc Dd Ee Ff Gg Hh Ii Jj Kk Ll Mm

Activity

1 **Look and read. Match.** 📖

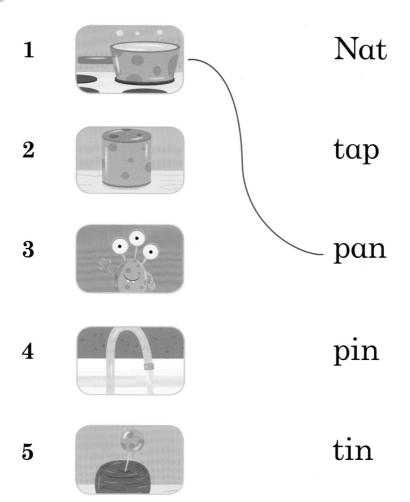

1   Nat

2   tap

3   pan

4   pin

5   tin

Nn Oo Pp Qq Rr Ss Tt Uu Vv Ww Xx Yy Zz

pin

Nat

pan

Nat

tap

Nat

tin

Nat

Nat

sit

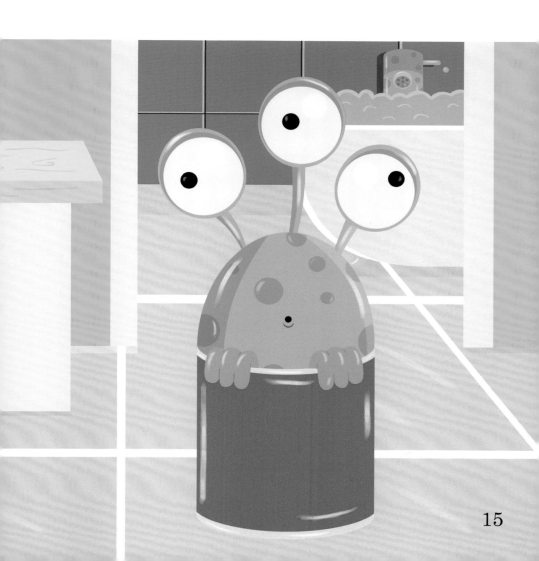

Ladybird Readers

Is it Nat?

Read the story

Now, read the story in full sentences.
Practice using the sight words.

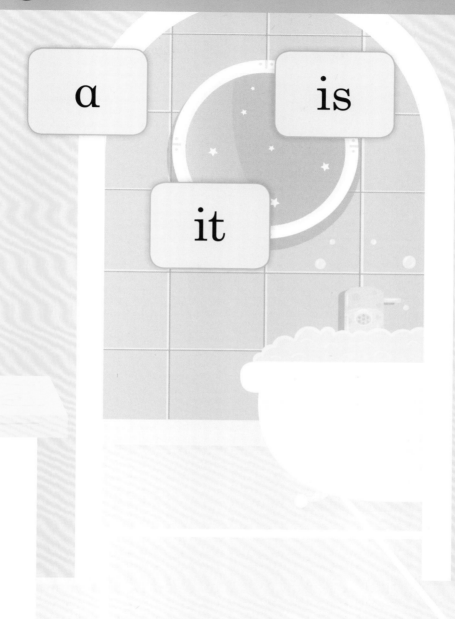

a

is

it

Is it a pin?

It is Nat.

Is it a pan?

It is Nat.

Is it a tap?

It is Nat.

Is it a tin?

It is Nat.

Sit, Nat!

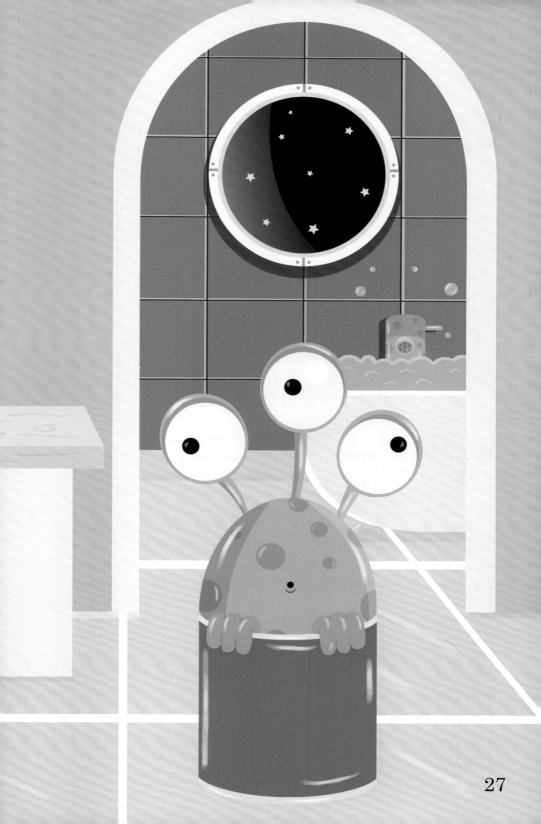

Activities

2 **Look and read. Color in.** 📖

pan	tin	pin

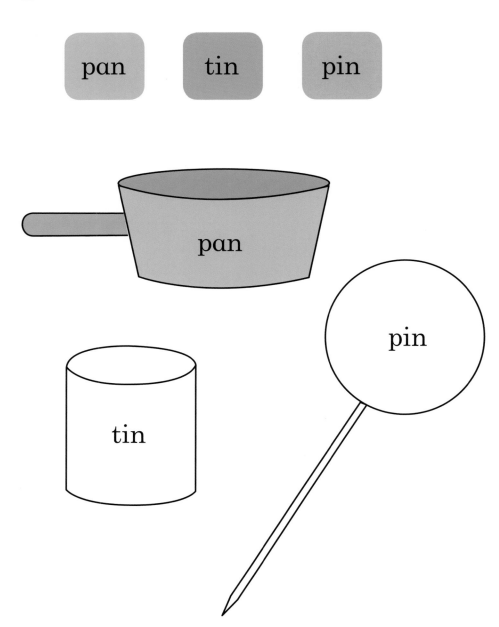

pan

pin

tin

3 **Find and circle the sight words.**

is it a

sdfjkl(is)bnmrewolkjitpomawefsislknvitdcwufgaklpz

Assessment

4 **Look and read.**
Write the correct letters.

p	i	a	t

1  Is it a ..p.. in?

2  It is N........t.

3  Is it a ....ap?

4  Is it a t........n?

5  Is it a ....an?

5 **Write the sight words on the lines.**

a	it	is

1  Is it _a_ pan?

2  Is _____ a tin?

3  Is it _____ pin?

4 It _____ Nat.

Starter

Alphabet Book

978–0–241–39367–3

Is it Nat?

978–0–241–39368–0

Nat Sits

978–0–241–39369–7

Top Dog and Pompom

978–0–241–39370–3

Top Dog is Sick

978–0–241–39371–0

The Fun Run

978–0–241–39372–7

Gus is Hot!

978–0–241–39373–4

Jazz the Vet

978–0–241–39374–1

Vick the Vet

978–0–241–39375–8

Dash and Thud

978–0–241–39376–5

Big Bad Bash

978–0–241–39377–2

The Big Fish

978–0–241–39379–6

The Big Ship

978–0–241–39380–2

Martin and Lorna

978–0–241–39381–9

Farmer Carl

978–0–241–39382–6

The Big Dipper

978–0–241–39383–3

The Silver Ring

978–0–241–39384–0

LADYBIRD BOOKS

UK | USA | Canada | Ireland | Australia
India | New Zealand | South Africa

Ladybird Books is part of the Penguin Random House group of companies
whose addresses can be found at global.penguinrandomhouse.com.
www.penguin.co.uk   www.puffin.co.uk   www.ladybird.co.uk

PENGUIN
Random House
UK

First published 2017. This edition published 2019
001

Copyright © Ladybird Books Ltd, 2017

Printed in China

A CIP catalogue record for this book is available from the British Library

ISBN: 978–0–241–39368–0

All correspondence to:
Ladybird Books
Penguin Random House Children's
80 Strand, London WC2R 0RL

MIX
Paper from
responsible sources
FSC® C018179

FSC
www.fsc.org